BY THE SAME AUTHOR

GROWING ORCHIDS AT YOUR WINDOWS
BROMELIADS
FLOWERING HOUSE PLANTS
BEGONIAS, INDOORS AND OUT
RARE ORCHIDS FOR HOME AND GREENHOUSE

Gardens Under Glass

THE MINIATURE GREENHOUSE
IN BOTTLE, BOWL OR DISH

JACK KRAMER

SIMON AND SCHUSTER · NEW YORK

THIRD PRINTING

SBN 671-20107-7
LIBRARY OF CONGRESS CATALOG CARD NUMBER: 71-79633
DESIGNED BY EVE METZ
MANUFACTURED IN THE UNITED STATES OF AMERICA

CONTENTS

5

CONTENTS

Gardens Under Glass

PHOTO: OWENS-ILLINOIS GLASS CO.

1 · Miniature Greenhouses

WHEN WE THINK of gardens under glass, we usually think of greenhouses or conservatories protected from the outside and with controlled conditions inside. The glass gardens in this book are miniature versions of these larger buildings. Any arrangement of plants in glass is a miniature garden. The container may be large, like a five-gallon water bottle, or as small as a mason jar. Whether it is called a bottle garden, a terrarium, or a Wardian case, whether it is completely enclosed or partially open, it is a living landscape with diminutive plants. These gardens are pretty pictures framed in their containers and viewed through glass. Such a garden is like looking at a store window, and everyone likes to do that. The glass sets it apart from the rest of the world.

When I moved from a house in California to a small apartment in Chicago, space was limited and windows were obscured by tall buildings allowing little light for growing house plants. Yet I knew I had to garden indoors. I turned to tiny gardens in their own little glass-enclosed world. What a fascinating hobby! I found I could view nature with even more interest close up in lilliputian gardens that require little space and little care.

There is practically no limit to the plants that can be grown in glass gardens. While some hobbyists specialize in ferns and tiny creeping plants, I have successfully planted azaleas and roses, cacti and succulents, palms, orchids, and even carnivorous plants. These gardens offer people an opportunity to use their hands and their imaginations to create hundreds of different kinds of landscapes. There is no need to carry heavy sacks of soil, caring for the gardens takes virtually no time, and searching for the right glass container or decorative dish—cider flagon, candy jar, chemist's flask—is treasure-hunt fun.

Here, then, is a fascinating and easy way to grow plants for young or old, including those with little time or those who do not have the strength to cope with full-size gardens. This gardening can be done by the busy executive or the housewife with little time to spare, or by a youngster with many other interests. We all can find satisfaction in watching plants flourish before our eyes, in having segments of nature at our fingertips. Gardens under glass offer almost ideal growing conditions for hundreds of small plants. Whether the garden is under a glass dome, in a hanging translucent bowl, in a bottle or in a brandy snifter, whether it is filled with native woodland plants or house plants, it is a living landscape in miniature that adds charms to any room.

Many plants—marantas, fittonias, ferns, cissus—grow better in a completely covered glass garden than in an ordinary room. They are shielded from fluctuating temperatures and drafts, and the conservation of moisture inside the container supplies their main requirement—high humidity. And in an enclosed garden there is little possibility of insect attack.

The glass garden that is not completely enclosed, such as a brandy snifter or bubble bowl, is a haven for plants that prefer less humidity and still need an evenly moist soil at all times. Whether you choose a partly open or a closed container, once it is planted care is at a minimum. Occasional pruning and picking off dead flowers are necessary, but daily watering, temperature adjustment and humidity are no longer your concern. The very nature of the garden furnishes these basic needs. Sometimes it is not necessary to water gardens under glass for months or even years.

WHAT TO GROW

Selection is vital with these plantings. It takes many plants to make an attractive landscape; select species that grow well together under the same conditions. Ferns, selaginellas and fittonias appreciate the high humidity of an enclosed garden. Some orchids and bromeliads flourish in aquariums or bowls. Even cacti and succulents can be grown in bottoms of glass percolators or candy jars without lids.

In glass gardens you can grow exotic greenhouse plants like anthuriums and jewel orchids that would perish at a window in an ordinary pot. Rare species of alocasias and philodendrons are other possibilities. They can glorify any room in the protection of a glass container. Large bowls or terrariums planted with rich soil offer limitless opportunities to grow flowering plants like miniature geraniums, roses and azaleas.

Certain plants are best suited to certain containers. A vertical sansevieria needs the height of a tall dome. Peperomias and other creeping plants look good in shallow containers, while palms and ferns with graceful fronds are certainly lovely in round bottles or bowls.

TOOLS

The first thing I discovered about gardens in glass was that growing these was quite different from growing house plants in pots. Because of the nature of the containers—some bottles and jars have very small openings—tools are needed that will help you to plant within a confined space. An 8-inch-diameter candy jar or goldfish bowl may have a 5-inch opening; getting your hand inside to set plants in place is difficult or impossible. I tried wooden chopsticks for a while, but they were not long enough for tall jars and bottles; neither were basting forks. I finally devised an implement made from a 14-inch length of galvanized wire (⅛-inch wire, obtainable at hardware stores). With pliers I bent one end of the wire to form a circular loop about one inch in diameter. The circle is not completely closed, and the opening permits the crown of the plant to be slipped into the loop and then lowered into the soil. To tamp down the soil around the base of the plant, I use another piece of wire with a tiny metal disk (about one inch in diameter) soldered to the end of the wire—much like a ski pole. Another idea for a planting tool, and a very good one, is a gadget (sold at hardware stores) called a "pickup tool." This is a flexible 24-inch wire with a retractable claw device at one end operated by a plunger at the other end. It costs about a dollar and is perfect for placing plants in soil.

Although aluminum foil can be fashioned into a funnel for pouring soil into containers, a small kitchen funnel is better. A rubber watering syringe is necessary for moistening soil without disturbing plants and an artist's 5-inch "X-Acto" cutting knife with a single-edged razor blade on the end (at art supply stores) is excellent for cutting and pruning plants in small gardens. In larger gardens, trim plants with the pickup tool.

To clean glass surfaces, use a lintless cloth and carborundum powder (at hardware stores). Kitchen cleansers and scouring powders contain abrasives that can scratch glass. While commercial window-cleaning products with ammonia can be used, the fumes are harmful to some plants and you must wait a few days before planting. Mix a small amount (½ teaspoon) of carborundum powder with enough water to make a paste. Smear this over the glass and allow it to dry. It is dry when you see a pink coating on the glass. Wipe clean with a lintless cloth.

No matter how carefully you plant the garden, when you finish there may be soil particles and smudges on the glass. Carborundum paste leaves a protective coating on the glass, so, using a narrow-beaked watering can, merely pour water down the sides of the container to remove soil particles. No other cleaning is necessary.

14

SOIL

Using a sterilized soil for glass gardens will deter soil pests, bacteria or weeds. (Actually, I do not always object to the weeds that occasionally appear. Sometimes they enhance the landscape; other times they do not, and I remove them.) Sterilized soil can be bought in packages at nurseries. If you cannot find it, you can sterilize soil by putting it, dry, through a sieve with ⅛-inch mesh into a saucepan of water. Use enough water to moisten the soil. Do not pack it down. Put the saucepan on the stove and turn up the heat until the water boils and then simmer for a few minutes. Be prepared for an unpleasant odor; it is part of the job but the results are worth it. Then pour the soil on a baking tin or other flat surface and let it dry. Or put moistened soil in a roasting pan for two hours at 200° F. Then mix soil with peat moss and sand in desired proportions. Add some finely crushed perlite or other porous stones and some charcoal granules to keep the soil sweet.

My standard potting mix for most plants is:

one part sand

one part loam (well balanced soil, not too heavy or too light in weight and easily crumbled)

one part leaf mold or peat moss.

To this mix, add more sand for cacti and succulents, more loam for moisture-loving plants like ferns or mosses.

A word about packaged soils: they are available in small amounts, a convenience to apartment dwellers, and they certainly can be used for glass gardens. However, be choosy about them. Some of the packaged soils are heavy in texture and tend to become somewhat muddy after they are watered a few times. The soil should be porous and have a flaky texture. If it is heavy (run your fingers through it) add some sand and leaf mold to it.

Do not use soilless mixes for glass gardens; they do not contain any nutrients, and constant feeding of plants is necessary when these mixtures are used. This becomes a complicated procedure with miniatures that you want to keep small.

GLASS GARDENS FOR CHILDREN

It seems that children are not usually interested in pot plants at windows, but they are enchanted with tiny plants grown under glass. They take delight in creating their own landscapes and watching them grow month by month. In a confined area, growth of plants can be easily observed.

A goldfish bowl or a wide-mouthed jar are good containers to start the young gardener on his way, for the opening of the container is large and planting is easy. Let your child keep the garden in his room so he can watch the daily progress of the plants. Carnivorous plants—Venus flytrap and pitcher plants —intrigue children, and these are good selections to start with (see Chapter 6).

After your child is successful with the simple garden, let him try the bottle garden, which is more challenging. Give him the tools and materials and let him go to work. It is an inexpensive way for him to learn about nature, and besides, it will keep him busy for hours.

PLANTING BOTTLE GARDENS

Glass gardens can be planted in a variety of receptacles. We will discuss the different kinds of containers and where you can find them in the next chapter. Now we would like to describe how to plant a bottle garden, which means any sort of narrow-necked receptacle such as a cider jug, a decanter or a chemist's flask. The same planting principles apply to other glass gardens. However, with bowls, wide-necked jars and aquariums, special tools are generally not necessary. The openings of these containers are usually large enough for your hand, so it is easy to put plants in place.

To prepare a bottle garden for planting, cover the base of the container with tiny stones mixed with charcoal granules. Put in a very small amount of peat moss. Tip the bottle from side to side so the peat covers the stones. Then, with a funnel, add soil. Be sure it is dry so it will flow through the funnel into position without spattering the sides of the container. With the pusher tool (described on page 14) make holes in the soil to receive each plant. Put the looped wire around the collar of the plant (or use the pickup tool, page 14) and set the plant roots about ½ inch deep into the soil, or so that all roots are covered by the soil. Now here is where the gymnastics come in. If you are using the pickup tool it is simple to remove it and leave the plant in position. With the homemade looped wire, some practice is necessary. Move the loop slightly to the right or left until it is free of the base of the plant and then carefully lift it from the bottle. Smooth soil over the roots with the "tamp-down" tool (also on page 14). Now, with a small sable-hair artist's paintbrush, brush excess dirt off plant foliage. Then funnel water slowly into the garden; the soil should be moist but never soggy.

After planting, set the garden in a semishaded place. In about a week, move it into light or sun according to the requirements of the plants. With bottle gardens, moisture does not escape and water is needed only occasionally. If the soil is soggy and too much moisture condenses and collects on the glass, mildew and root rot may occur in plants. Merely uncover the garden—remove the lid or take out the stopper—for an hour a day to allow the inside to dry out somewhat.

Another way to start a bottle garden is to sprinkle some seed on the soil bed. As seedlings grow, pull out the smaller ones; keep one or perhaps two small plants growing. This method is actually harder to follow than assembling a complete garden with tiny plants. It takes much time to remove the unwanted seedlings and there is always the danger of accidentally pulling up the focal plant.

Large bottles—water jugs, glass chemical containers—are generally placed upright. However, if there is a proper stand for them, they can be put on their sides. Decide before you put

Charcoal granules, put through funnel, make a 1-inch bed at bottom of bottle.

plants into the bottle how it will be placed on the table or windowsill.

With bottles with small openings, removing faded flowers and decayed leaves and twigs is a tedious operation. Yet it must be done. Use the long wire with the circular loop on the end, or the pickup tool, or the artist's "X-Acto" knife, and proceed carefully, trying not to disturb the plantings. It takes time to keep a bottle garden neat and handsome but it is well worth doing.

After a few years, a bottle garden may become overgrown even though small plants were chosen at the start. Replanting is necessary. Do not try to dump the contents out of the bottle. Each plant must be lifted out with a tool. What went in small may now be large. To remove the plant without harming it, draw it up by the roots with the wire tool or pickup tool; let the foliage bunch together and pass through the neck of the bottle. Now let the soil in the bottle dry out completely; then turn the bottle upside down, remove the soil and wash the container thoroughly.

Planting instructions are given in Chapter 2 for various other types of glass gardens.

18

Plant is lifted with pickup tool to be placed in bottle (top).

Plant is released by pickup tool and inserted in soil (lower left).

Soil around base of plant is tamped down with wooden stick (lower right).

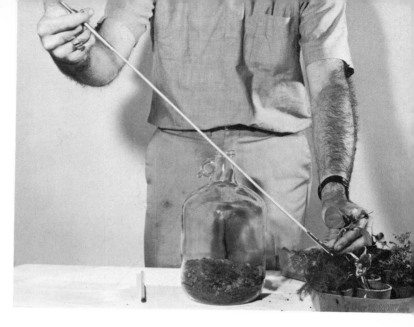

ALL PHOTOS: JOYCE R. WILSON

In watering bottle garden, tilt funnel and pour water slowly down sides of container so plants are not disturbed.

CARE OF GARDENS UNDER GLASS

Plants in glass containers depend on a balanced environment of the right humidity, temperature and light. They also need a good chance to grow, so give them room; do not crowd them. Check the soil frequently to see that it is neither soggy nor too dry; it should be evenly moist. A soggy soil coupled with too much heat or darkness is an invitation to fungus disease. Keep gardens on the cool side (about 56°F., at night) and lift the lid or cover from time to time so air can circulate in the growing area. Keep the garden clean of faded flowers and decayed twigs and foliage. Pinch or trim or snip plants ruthlessly to keep them attractive and compact. I assure you that trimming does not harm the plant. New branches and new growth will be plump and fresh. Stop pinching only if you see buds on flowering plants.

It is easy to keep plants trimmed in domes or in bubble bowls or glass snifters; a manicure scissors does the job. But trimming

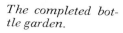
The completed bottle garden.

PHOTOS: JOYCE R. WILSON

plants in a bottle garden with a long neck and a small opening is a magician's trick. My magic wand is the pickup tool with the retractable claw to pluck off faded flowers and leaves. Or you might try the gadget that plucks olives and pickles from jars. It works on the same principle and is sold at hardware stores.

I see no reason to fertilize plants in glass; you want them to stay small, so why try to speed up the growing process? Plants in glass gardens stay in good health for many years without feeding.

2·Glass Containers

THERE IS something fascinating about looking at plants through glass. They become a living landscape in a world of their own. Growing plants in glass containers is not new; the Wardian case became popular more than one hundred years ago. It was named for the English botanist Nathaniel B. Ward, who discovered that many plants would thrive for years in stoppered bottles or closed glass cases.

The sphinx moth was actually responsible for the Wardian case. To make a study of the moth emerging from its chrysalis, Dr. Ward put it in a closed bottle. In a few weeks he noticed condensation on the inside of the glass running down the sides of the bottle into the earth. And he was astonished to see seedling ferns and grasses growing in the bottle—the same plants he had tried, without success, to grow in his backyard in the smoky atmosphere of London. He allowed the plants to remain in the covered bottles, where they flourished for almost four years with never a drop of water.

Dr. Ward immediately started growing a wide range of plants in glass cases with considerable success. And so began a whole new way of easy gardening with interesting plants—plants that would never survive the average conditions of a home. Wardian cases were built in many different styles and sizes. Some were small, for table decoration, while others were large, for bay windows, and some were used to transport plants from distant lands.

PHOTO: JOYCE R. WILSON

PHOTO BY AUTHOR

PHOTO: JOYCE R. WILSON

Upper left: Variegated ivy lives for many months in a chemist's flask.

Upper right: Chamaedorea elegans and a peperomia in an old-fashioned candy jar.

Bottom left: A 5-gallon pickle jar makes a glass house for a croton, baby tears and wild strawberry.

A container for a glass garden can be anything from an inexpensive fishbowl to an elegant decanter or a brandy snifter. The glass containers patterned after apothecary jars are at present very popular. Many household items can also be put to use.

23

Glass cake covers, bottoms of glass coffee percolators, and empty distilled-water bottles are a few examples. The principle is the same with all glass gardens: to produce moisture by evaporation which condenses on the sides and trickles down into the soil.

Today, with the variety of glass containers available, the choice of the housing is as interesting as the selection of plants. An entirely new world of gardening is at our fingertips.

BOWLS AND GLOBES

I suppose every household has been through the goldfish phase. When the kids get tired of the idea, let them set up a glass garden. The octagonal flat-sided fishbowls make fine containers. They are inexpensive and they come in several different sizes. To prepare the bowl for planting, spread some shredded sphagnum moss on the bottom, add about ½ inch of aquarium gravel for drainage and some charcoal granules to keep the soil sweet. Then pour in soil to a depth of several inches in proportion to the size of the bowl. Use soil appropriate to the kinds of plants being grown. Ferns prefer an acid mix, cacti and succulents need sand, and orchids and bromeliads need pockets of fir bark or osmunda.

When filling the container with soil, try not to dirty the inside of the glass—with wide-mouthed bowls this is not too much of a problem, but with narrow-mouthed jars and bottles, once the glass is dirty it is difficult to clean.

In bowls and globes, place plants sparsely; they need room to grow. Open-top gardens, although protected with glass sides, still need periodic watering. Covered bowls need less water, and some can go without moisture for many months. Frequency of watering and the quantity of water depend on the size of the bowl and other environmental factors. However, as with all plantings, the soil should never be allowed to become bone dry. Test the soil with your fingers as you do with ordinary pot plants.

I have an antique kerosene lamp I discovered in a salvage shop; the globe was missing but at an electrical supplier's I lo-

Ivy and Chinese evergreen flourish in this covered glass dish.

cated a clear 16-inch globe. This gave me the idea for a unique garden. The globe has a top and bottom opening for the glass chimney of the lamp. I set the globe in a bed of sand in a shallow dish to keep it upright. Then with soil and plants I made a garden that always brings comments from guests. Of course, I had to return to the supplier to get another globe for the lamp.

Glass globes are now at electrical companies in several sizes. I prefer the 14-inch diameter. These globes, manufactured for the lighting trade, have a 2- to 3-inch opening, and while planting them may take patience, beautiful arrangements can be made. Once again, the bottom of the globe must be embedded in

Peperomia and ivy are the base of this attractive arrangement.

25

sand to keep it upright. If you want something different for an underwater scene for water plants, select a globe with a partially textured finish. A glass cylinder is another idea for vertical arrangements; be sure to buy a cylinder that has a wide opening. One with a 10-inch diameter works fine for plantings.

AQUARIUMS

Don't throw away a leaky aquarium. One of my first glass gardens came out of sheer desperation. I tried in vain to seal the leaks in my aquarium with putty, but I was unsuccessful. A neighbor who owned a florist's shop suggested I grow tiny plants in the tank, and this endeavor succeeded.

Leaky aquariums can sometimes be found at salvage shops. The tanks lend themselves beautifully to many different types of landscape—desert, woodland, and so on. The soil, at least three inches deep, should be built up into gentle slopes or natural mounds—a flat terrain is dull. After putting in the plants, you can add stones or pebbles for paths. Baby tears or other creeping species make a lovely carpet of green, and they accent hills and valleys. Use figurines discreetly—bridges, statues, and so on. Be sure they really belong in the setting. Put larger and bolder plants in the background and between them place not-so-tall foliage and flowering species.

My best tank gardens have been in ten-gallon aquariums measuring about 16″ × 20″ and with enough space for a dozen well-chosen plants. A glass store will cut a sheet of glass for the top; have it cut two inches shorter than the tank opening so air can circulate in the garden.

FLASKS AND JARS

Chemists' flasks make attractive greeneries but they are difficult to plant. Try these only after you have mastered other glass gardens. The long narrow neck—usually 1 to 2 inches

26

A variety of native plants in a terrarium makes a delightful woodland garden.

wide—makes this a challenging project. A patient hand and infinite care are needed to be successful. And too, some of the flasks have a rounded bottom so keeping them upright involves setting them in a dish of sand or some other device. Flasks are available in several sizes, and if you tackle this garden, go all the way. Use unique plants such as miniature orchids or carnivorous species. To those who admire it, it will seem that you labored for days to complete this garden gem. And, indeed, you will.

There are all kinds of jars and bottles to use for glass gardens —from cider jugs to peanut-butter jars to purified-water containers (see planting instructions for bottle gardens, pages 16-18). Search your supermart; you will be surprised at what you can find if you can visualize the containers empty and filled with living plants. Some have wide mouths, others narrow openings; all can be planted. So, if the shape and size of the container suit your fancy, get to work. Of course you may find yourself, as I did, with five gallons of dill pickles and four pounds of peanut butter, but there are always hungry children around my house.

The commercial glass containers come in many sizes and shapes; the traditional pear-shaped and Ming urn covered jars are still seen, and new designs keep appearing.

A new saw advertised in garden magazines deserves mention here. This saw cuts glass with ease and permits a new approach to gardening under glass. Simply saw the jug at the desired height, plant the garden in a dish and then put the cut jug over it. For me, the sawing method is better than the old-fashioned burning-string procedure, which I think is hazardous. However, if you do not have the saw and you want to cut a jug, proceed as follows: Soak a piece of string in lighter fluid and wrap it around the jug where you want it cut. Light the string and let the flame burn out. Then quickly dunk the jug in cold water. You should then be able to break off the unwanted part. You may have to repeat the whole procedure a few times to get a clean break. And even a clean break has razor-sharp edges. Cover them with masking tape or have them ground smooth at a local glass shop.

DECANTERS AND BRANDY SNIFTERS

Crystal decanters for wine or liquor, while rarely cheap, make elegant greeneries. Some are square, others round; they come in varying sizes and they generally have a glass stopper. These are fine containers for a few plants. I think it is extravagant to buy new ones for gardens, but I have found decanters in salvage shops at reasonable prices. These gardens are handsome when placed on a coffee table or an end table but out of character, to my eye, on windowsills.

The large brandy-snifter garden so often seen in florists' shops is attractive but hardly unusual when compared with the newer containers. In my view, the container is just as important as the plants, and brandy snifters seem an easy answer rather than an artistic one. They are best left to their original purpose—drinking brandy—and that's good too.

TERRARIUMS TO BUY OR TO MAKE

Any plastic or glass container filled with plants can be called a terrarium. There are many commercial terrariums for small gardens. Some have plastic tops with waterproof footed-metal bases; others are metal and glass. The most popular sizes are 11″ × 15″, 8″ ×12″, and 13″ × 16″; these cases accommodate about a dozen plants. An all-glass cube with an interior space for plants is another idea. Keep these units at eye level so it is easy to see the plants in them. The new Crystalite indoor greenhouse is another good housing; it is 18″ × 24″ and comes with a wick-fed automatic watering tray.

If the commercial greenhouse does not have drainage facilities—and the one I bought several years ago did not—bore small holes in the bottom metal tray so water can escape, and set a shallow pan under the unit.

It is also possible to make a case. Find a flat box about 5 inches deep of convenient size, say 12″ × 16″. A slatted box will allow water to escape; if the box is solid, drill ⅛-inch holes in the bottom so water can escape. A glass shop will cut panes to size for the sides; have the top piece cut larger than the case to serve as a cover. Set the four panes for the sides vertically in the box; fill with some soil to hold the glass in place. Now use Dow Corning's Silastic to seal the edges. Plant directly into the wooden box. Compartmented cases can be made, too, to house many different kinds of miniature gardens or, if you want to keep it simple, merely use an inverted plastic sweater box over a wood or metal tray.

FLOWERS IN GLASS

We are all fond of freshly cut flowers but we know they simply do not last for more than a few days. But there is a way to have roses or carnations, camellias or orchids stay in vibrant color for several weeks. Put them in a glass container with a lid.

Bubble bowls, apothecary jars, even egg-shaped vases in colors are now at florists' shops. Cut flowers encased in glass become colorful jewels that make unique table decorations.

Put a small amount of water in the bottom of a glass bowl and then place a single flower, or perhaps two or three of them, so that they float on the water. You will have to cut the stems short so the flowers rest directly on the water. In the protection of a glass container, the flowers do not deteriorate and the small amount of water in the bowl prevents them from drying out.

While almost any flower can be used in a glass bowl, large blooms like roses, carnations and camellias show to better advantage than small flowers, which are apt to appear lost in a glass world. I have had roses stay fresh for almost a month in a handsome apothecary jar.

Not to be confused with fresh flowers in glass are hermetically sealed crystal containers with preserved flowers. These are handsome arrangements of flowers that are secured at the base of the bowl in a cement-type mixture. This type of glass garden lasts for years. Wild flowers, garden flowers and all kinds of plant materials are used, and while to me they are not as exciting as fresh flowers, they do have an intimate charm.

At one time, flowers completely submerged in liquid in glass bowls were popular. A chemical solution was used to preserve the blooms, but at intervals the chemical had to be replaced, and this could only be done by sending the glass bowl back to the manufacturer—a tedious chore. While these glass specialties are still available, they have a certain fakeness that does not appeal to everyone.

Cut flowers can last for weeks in a covered glass container.

3·Gardens Under Domes

ANY GROUP of living plants in an interesting container is a dish garden. The scene can become your own miniature greenhouse when you place a dome over it. A few potted plants lined up on a windowsill or a solitary plant on a table simply do not have the appeal of a group of well-chosen plants under glass.

A dome garden can be a scene—a miniature replica of nature whether it be woodland, Oriental or tropical in theme. Deciding on a dominant theme for the garden is more interesting than having it a hodgepodge of plants. It is a challenge, too, because each little plant is important to the whole. Miniature compositions are always more difficult to create and are under closer scrutiny than large-scale ones.

PLACEMENT OF GARDENS

Place dome gardens in any room in the home—on a bedside table, a mantel or a coffee table, in a bookcase shelf or on a windowsill. Miniature gardens are for accent; they are like pictures on a wall to decorate a room. Do not fret if they do not last a lifetime. They will outlast a dozen roses or a gift plant, and usually cost much less.

However, if you happen to be penurious like me and want

them to last a long time, keep them near windows where there is some light.

GLASS DOMES (BELLS)

Glass domes for covering microscopes and stuffed birds and other memorabilia are available from a few manufacturers. Or you can hunt for them at antique shops. These domes of high-quality glass, placed on a suitable dish, make ideal gardens. The trick with dome gardening is to find the bowl or dish for the bottom to suit the dome, or vice versa. The dome must fit just inside the rim of the bowl without allowing a gap so that earth is exposed to air. Pottery or china or stone bowls or dishes are all possibilities; whenever I see a handsome one that I think will do for a garden, I buy it. (It can always be used for something else if it doesn't fit.)

Domes come with or without wooden platforms; these are not necessary for the garden. Dome sizes range from 3 inches in diameter and 6 inches in height to 13 inches in diameter and 27 inches in height (see list of suppliers at end of book).

Plastic domes, while not as attractive as glass ones, can also be used for miniature landscapes. These are generally found at stores as covers for cheese-serving trays. These plastic domes are usually low and round, and a suitable dish must be found for them. You can have a small metal tray made that fits the dome circumference, but this is costly, so, once again, it's probably best to search for pottery or stone dishes. I have never seen the low dome design in glass. With the plastic dome, moisture collecting on the inside walls does not run down into the soil as freely as it runs off smooth glass. There is, however, an easy way to help nature along. Shake the plastic dome occasionally to loosen the beads of moisture. Use tiny plants for these plastic-

Opposite page: A glass dome and an interesting ceramic container combine to make a miniature greenhouse where plants will live for a long time with almost no care. PHOTO: JOYCE R. WILSON

32

enclosed gardens; there really isn't too much height, and the garden becomes unattractive when plants scrape the roof.

I have a favorite garden under a glass cake cover that is 6 inches high and 10 inches across. This is an ideal dome for tiny plants, with just enough height and area. And the top is slightly convex, allowing more vertical growing space.

DISHES AND CONTAINERS

The dish for the dome garden must accommodate the glass bell or dome. The diameter of the opening of the dome dictates the size of the dish for it. Search for one that has a lip or flange to hold the glass top; the dish must be deep enough for at least 3 inches of soil. There are suitable plants for all types of dishes and bowls, whether you choose one with an ornate fluted or scrolled motif or a plain or colored dish.

The pedestal dish is especially good for dome gardens. It raises the scene off the ground and really puts it on display.

Some dishes have drainage holes in the bottom—shallow bonsai containers, for example—but the majority of containers do not. Dishes without drainage holes—I warn you now—must be watered carefully and sparingly or the soil becomes a soggy mess. If it is possible, take the container to a glass shop and have some tiny holes bored in the bottom so water can escape. Some containers will crack in the drilling process, others will not. Once holes are drilled, find a suitable pan or clay saucer to set under the dish to catch water. If such a pan is aesthetically un- pleasing—and many times it is—water the glass garden in the sink. Let it drain a few minutes and place it on a cork mat to avoid moisture stains on table surfaces.

As I have mentioned earlier, in gardening under glass there is the constant hazard of soggy soil and overwatered plants. Start right. Put in a good drainage bed of small pieces of broken flower pots, coarse sand and some charcoal granules. Then spread a layer of soil. Select the specific soil for the plants being grown (see Chapter 1).

A glass cake cover and a dish that exactly fits it make an unusual garden under glass.

PLANTING A DOME GARDEN

Before you plant a dome garden, set the potted plants in the dish and move them around until you hit on the right placement. If you buy plants only in 2- or 3-inch-diameter pots—and you should—this is a simple procedure. Set the largest plant off to one side to create an accent and put small plants around the base. For a striking effect, use the accent plant in a bed of white sand or colored gravel.

Trim plants, still in their pots, so they have an attractive sculptural growth. For instance, the small pomegranate (punica granatum nana) is a stellar tiny garden subject; it can be pruned to the desired shape without harm to it. Use bold foliage like peperomias against the graceful fronds of a fern, a feathery yellow-green asparagus sprengeri (emerald fern) in front of a dark green bold plant like kalanchoe Blossfeldiana.

A flat design with a level grading of earth is dull; give

35

your garden hills and valleys. Shape the contour of the soil so that it is interesting and pleasing. Make the front of the garden low and mound the soil in the rear. Set a plateau and pieces of flat shale in a corner. There are many variations; don't be afraid to use your imagination.

To plant the garden, gently ease the plants from their individual pots (it helps to tap the pot first against a firm surface) and set each plant in place. Firm the soil around the collar of each plant to support it. Last to go in are trailing plants, ground-cover and gravel chips, if you are using them.

Many tiny plants like pellaea rotundifolia are charming grown in crevices in small rocks. It is all right to use accessories like little pieces of rock or some figurines or small ceramic objects, but do not overdo it. A note of whimsy is fine in some gardens but too many props give a cluttered look. While some people like reflecting pools made with mirrors, to me they are just too cute. So are most cheap figurines.

CARE OF DOME GARDENS

Try to keep the soil evenly moist at all times; this is not an easy matter. What looks moist on top may be bone dry at the bottom, and many times the bottom may be a soggy mess while the top layer of soil is dry. I poke my finger deep into the soil, trying not to dislodge any plant, to test for moisture. Then I know if I should water the garden.

When you water, do not dump it into the dish. You will dislodge soil and plants. Pour water gently into the dish from a spout can.

Spray foliage from time to time to keep it fresh and lush. Pick off faded flowers and dead leaves. Keep the piece attractive. If plants are getting straggly and touching the glass, trim them ruthlessly. I have no qualms about doing this; most house plants are tough and recover quickly with fresh growth. Fragile though they may seem, plants want to live. Cutting off dead blooms in a dome garden is easy because the dome can be removed.

Peperomia and baby tears are at home under a glass percolator bottom.

Left: A copper container and a graceful dome make an appealing glass garden for a flourishing ivy plant.

Generally, living-room temperatures are fine for gardens although I find that many of the lilliputian landscapes prefer coolness, say 55° F. at night, rather than warmth. Because of its glass cover, a miniature greenhouse is never plagued by the low humidity that desiccates most house plants. And if there is too much moisture in the garden, merely remove the glass top for a few hours or prop it with a matchstick so air can enter.

If by chance you have erred in the selection of plants and they get too large and outgrow their confines, remove them and pot them separately as window plants. Then start again and hope that your dome gardens will remain small and beautiful for many months.

37

4 · The Plants

WHILE THE CONTAINER is important for miniature gardens under glass, it is the plants that make the garden. Don't rush out and buy anything. Pick and choose—there are many beautiful miniatures but there are also some undesirable ones. Some grow rapidly, others are naturally straggly and not fit for the unique container you have selected for the garden. And, too, different plants have different light requirements. If proper selection of plants is made at the start, your miniature garden will be with you for years.

A multitude of miniature plants, and the seedlings of mature ones, can be grown in glass gardens. There are tiny trees, flowering plants, foliage gems, water plants and even herbs. Try to select plants that grow slowly and choose species that are compatible when grown together. Ferns and mosses need a rich soil and shade. Flowering plants require a few hours of daily sun. Most succulents and cacti need lots of sun.

A great many plants can be bought at local nurseries or florists; even the smallest florist's shop has a house-plant section where you will find plants for your glass greeneries. Of course, plants such as miniature orchids, geraniums and begonias are best purchased from mail-order suppliers who specialize in these plants. If possible, order in spring and fall. Summer heat desiccates plants, and in winter there is always the possibility of receiving frozen plants.

38

FERNS

I mention ferns first because, with their lovely fronds, they are superior plants for backgrounds. Most plants do not have their curving lines. And the majority of ferns thrive in a covered garden, where they are greener and healthier than if grown uncovered at windows. I know; I have them in both places.

While it is desirable to choose true miniature ferns (to 8 inches) even larger species can be put into the garden. When young, they are small and do not grow rapidly. One of my favorite ferns is *Adiantum bellum*, a diminutive version of the maidenhair fern, with ruffled leaflets and wiry stems. Many ferns that are dormant in winter will usually grow all year in a glass garden. Grow plants in shade with coolness (58° F. at night); use a rich soil with plenty of humus. (For native ferns of the woods, see Chapter 6.)

Ferns for glass gardens.   PHOTO: MERRY GARDENS, CAMDEN, MAINE

Here are some ferns that grow easily in glass gardens:

Adiantum bellum—6-inch miniature version of maidenhair fern.

Adiantum hispidulum—lovely dark-green branching fronds.

Asplenium nidus (bird's nest fern)—young plants are fine for garden. They have leathery bright-green spatula-shaped leaves.

Cyrtomium falcatum (holly fern)—large but handsome; good for large glass case.

Nephrolepis exalta 'Verona'—dwarf Boston fern with pendulous lacy fronds.

Nephrolepis exaltata 'Childsii'—dwarf, with waxy green fronds. Slow-growing.

Pellaea rotundifolia (button fern)—dark stems with shiny round green leaves. Decorative.

Polystichum tsus simense—dwarf fern with delicate lacy fronds; good fill-in plant.

Pteris ensiformis 'Victoriae'—silver leaves margined with dark green.

CYCADS AND PALMS

Cycads are an ancient family of primitive plants found in Africa and Australia. They are graceful and delicate and they resemble ferns, but the crowns of leaves are borne from a central trunk similar to palm fronds. Plants are slow-growing and their form and grace make them highly desirable for glass gardens. While many of them are large plants, there are some excellent dwarf species.

Cycads are easier to grow than ferns and thrive in bright light with an evenly moist soil.

Some of the smaller palms also make fine subjects for glass

gardens. Like cycads, they are slow-growing and require little care. They are graceful, tough to kill and add charm to any indoor garden. Grow cycads and palms in bubble bowls or glass containers without covers.

Cycads

Cycas circinalis—ferny type with shiny dark-green leaves. Use young plants.

Cycas revoluta—sago palm; dark, shiny green leaves. Popular; easy to grow.

Macrozamia lucida—small; whitish-green leaves.

Zamia fischeri—dwarf with dark-green leaves.

Zamia furfuracea—foliage brownish-colored with hairs.

Palms

Caryota mitis (fishtail palm)—young plants are handsome with leaf wedges shaped like fishtails.

Chamaedorea elegans bella—dwarf, with graceful arching fronds.

Chamaerops humilis—never grows more than 30 inches; young plants ideal for glass case; fan-shaped blue-green foliage.

Cocos weddelliana (Syagrus weddeliana)—coco palm, with feathery yellow-green foliage.

Collinia elegans—dwarf; attractive narrow-leaved palm.

Reinhardtia gracilis gracilior (window palm)—window pattern in leaves. Unique.

FOLIAGE AND FLOWERING PLANTS

There is no end to foliage and flowering plants for the glass garden. There are crawlers, creepers, upright growers, all with a variety of leaf pattern and texture. Some are bold with thick leaves, others are delicate with lacy foliage. Many species have branching growth; others are compact and bushy. Several are true miniatures, growing only to about 12 inches and others are medium-sized plants that can be kept in bounds by pruning. The trailers and creepers are always good to use because they are easily cut to fit the confines of the garden.

Select plants carefully. The glass garden, whether it is in a bottle or under a dome in a dish, is a complete scene, and any plant that does not blend into the setting is quickly spotted.

It would be impossible to list all suitable plants here; I recommend those that have some interesting feature—shape, leaf texture or growth—and the ones that do best for me. Grow them in rich soil in average home temperatures. An asterisk denotes plants that require the high humidity of a covered garden.

For Semishade

Aglaonema pictum—one of the best foliage plants, with blue-green leaves splashed with silver. Somewhat large, but can be trimmed to desired shape and size.

Alternanthera Bettzickiana—a bright miniature with yellow, pink, red and green foliage. Group a few of these in one area for some concentrated color.

*Anthurium scherzerianum (flamingo plant)—attractive green leaves; red shiny bracts.

*Caladium—a group with many varieties well suited to diminutive landscapes. Try: *C. humboldtii*—small deep-green leaves marked with silver; 'Little Rascal'—lance-shaped wine-red foliage; or 'Twilight'—flaming pink leaves netted with green.

Caladium humboldtii, *a good choice for a miniature glass garden.*

These plants may die down in winter; if so, lift them from the garden.

Calathea bachemiana—not really a miniature but a lush plant with velvety gray-green leaves edged with dark green. Also handsome is *C. picturata argentea*—silver leaves etched in dark green.

Ceropegia cafforum—a climber with dark-green leaves, red underneath. Another dainty species is *C. Woodii* (rosary vine), with heart-shaped blue-green foliage with silver veins.

Chamaeranthemum igneum—tropical creeper with velvety bronze-brown leaves and pink veins.

Codiaeum variegata pictum (croton)—a bushy plant that will need pruning to keep it small. It has bright-green leaves spotted with yellow.

Columnea microphylla—a charming small gesneriad with tiny leaves and bright-red flowers; will climb or trail. Don't miss this one.

Cryptanthus bromelioides tricolor—one of the best small bromeliads, with rosettes of green leaves striped pink and white. *C. bivittatus (roseus picta)* bears bronze-pink foliage striped pale green.

Dionaea muscipula (Venus fly trap)—a carnivorous plant with curious growth; always causes comment.

Drosera rotundifolia—a tiny insect-eater with spoon-shaped growth covered with red hairs tipped with a sticky substance. Insect landing on plant is trapped and pulled into plant.

Episcia—spreading plant with velvety leaves in magnificent colors, with charming flowers. Select small species; many available.

Ficus radicans variegata—a dainty foliage creeper with silver-green leaves marked white. Also desirable is *F. repens pumila*, heart-shaped dark-green foliage; sends out discs that cling to glass.

Fittonia verschaffeltii (mosaic plant)—a creeper with irridescent foliage; grows slowly and remains dwarf size.

Hedera helix—a large group of delightful ivies, many well suited for the glass garden. Try: 'Buttercup'—golden-yellow leaves; 'California Gold'—pale-green leaves splashed yellow; 'Curlilocks'—apple-green leaves with ruffled edges; 'Glacier'—variegated triangular leaves; 'Needlepoint'—sharply cut leaves; 'Pixie'—branching miniature ivy.

Helxine soleirolii (baby tears)—one of the most refreshing wee creepers around with buttonlike bright-green leaves.

Malpighia coccigera (miniature holly)—glossy green leaves and pink flowers. Robust.

Manettia bicolor (firecracker vine)—a climbing vine that rarely fails to bear red and yellow flowers; after blooming, cut back to keep small.

Maranta oppenheimiana tricolor—a stellar foliage plant with glowing multicolored foliage.

Nerium oleander (oleander)—pink or white flowers on young plants.

Pandanus vietchi—striped yellow-and-green leaves; young plants are best.

44

Pilea involucrata *and* pilea repens.

Pellionia repens—a creeper with elliptical metal-green foliage; stays small.

Peperomia—a group of many miniatures, most with heart-shaped or oval leaves. Try: 'Little Fantasy'—silver-green and brown leaves; 'Pixie'—bright green; *P. rubella*—moss-green foliage.

*Pilea—a genus of fleshy creepers. *P. cadierei minima* (aluminum plant)—silver-green foliage; *P. depressa*—sea-green toothed leaves; *P. nummularifolia*—heart-shaped fuzzy green leaves; *P. repens*—tiny, round bronze foliage.

Sansevieria (snake plant)—some varieties are low growing; ideal for the glass garden. 'Hahni'—a spiral of broad dark-green leaves; 'Golden Hahni'—green leaves marked with yellow.

A varied group of peperomias.

For Sun (2 to 3 hours a day)

Azalea 'Gumpo'—a delightful small variety with frilled red flowers.

Bambusa nana—a grassy plant that needs severe pruning; use only a few shoots.

Bertolonia maculata—a miniature with dark-green, silver and red foliage very appealing.

Chlorophytum bitchetti—a trailer with green-and-yellow foliage; does well in glass garden. Cut and prune to desired size.

Chrysanthemum multicaule—bright-yellow flowers; for large case.

Coleus rehneltianus—a highly colored plant that can be kept small by pruning.

Crossandra infundibuliformis—a fine shiny green-leaved plant with crowns of orange flowers. Blooms young.

Dianthus glauca nana—not often seen, but satisfactory for the small glass garden. Bright pink flowers.

*Dracaena godseffiana—a slow-growing shrub with yellow-and-green foliage; can be kept small.

Exacum affine—a gentian that bears blue flowers.

Ixora fulgens—a floriferous plant; red flowers.

Kalanchoe Blossfeldiana—many varieties; small red flowers.

Rhipsalidopsis rosea *blooms cheerfully in a sunny glass garden.*

A colorful streptocarpus will add a gay note to a garden under glass.

Oxalis—a fine group with two excellent small species for glass gardens: *O. hedysaroides rubra* with bright golden flowers and *O. henrei* bearing tiny yellow blooms.

Rhipsalidopsis rosea—a robust small plant with splendid rose-pink flowers.

Saxifraga sarmentosa (strawberry geranium)—a favorite with round, hairy, silver-veined leaves. Bushy, always attractive.

Schizocentron elegans—(Spanish shawl)—a creeper with tiny leaves and purple blooms.

Streptocarpus—gesneriads that offer a great deal of color for little effort. Try: *S. Rexi*—pale orchid flowers with purple throat; and *S. saxorum*—lavender-white blooms.

MINIATURE GERANIUMS (PELARGONIUMS)

Miniature geraniums are worth their space in gold; they are always bright and cheerful, and if their cultural requirements are met, they grow for years. Use a mixture of equal parts of sand and garden soil for them, kept evenly moist at all times. The soil should be damp to the touch; don't let it get so dry that it is powdery. Sun is necessary for bloom, so put the glass garden in a south or east window. Geraniums do fine in temperatures from 60 to 70° F. in the daytime, with a ten-degree drop at night.

Most miniatures are compact and bushy if the growing tips

47

Dwarf geraniums will add brilliant color when placed in the miniature landscape.

are pinched off when the plants are young, and then again after they bloom. If you grow geraniums in covered gardens, be sure to lift the lid often to allow air to circulate in the area. Too much humidity is as bad as too little moisture in the air for these plants.

Some good miniature varietals are:

'Alcyone'—pink flowers.

'Aldebaran'—dark pink.

'Altair'—salmon pink.

'Antares'—red.

'Capella'—salmon pink.

'Fairy Tales'—white.

'Filigree'—salmon pink.

'Goblin'—red.

'Imp'—pink.

'Merope'—red.

'Meteor'—dark red.

'Pigmy'—red.

MINIATURE ROSES

Do you like roses? And have you always envied people with lovely rose gardens? Now the queen of flowers can be at your fingertips in a private glass garden. Miniature roses, tiny replicas of standard roses, are twice as enchanting in a glass world. Originally grown as indoor pot plants in Switzerland, these delicate beauties are now plentiful in this country. They have a long flowering season, are only 3 to 12 inches tall, and all in all are truly remarkable plants.

Because they suffer from the fluctuating temperatures of the average living room, they are ideal subjects for a closed case. But certainly such beauty does not come without attention. Keep vigil for pests and diseases. All faded flowers must be removed immediately. Be on constant alert for spider mites and aphids. Mildew and botrytis grow rapidly on decaying foliage or stems, so be sure to remove any debris from the soil. Keep soil moist but never soggy, and give roses sun; they will not flourish without it. Roses appreciate cool temperatures (60° F.).

Some good miniature varietals are:

'Baby Crimson'	'Red Imp'
'Bo Peep'	'Rosata'
'Cinderella'	'Scarlet Gem'
'Granada'	'Thumbelina'
'Mon Petit'	'Yellow Miniature'
'Pixie Gold'	

MINIATURE BEGONIAS

Miniature begonias are charmers that bear bright flowers in winter and spring. The plants grow slowly and need only minimum care to bloom. Use fine-textured soil to pot these begonias; pinch and prune them to form pleasing shapes. Keep begonias in bright light but out of sun. Some species will thrive in the protection of a closed dome, others need more air circulation. Many small begonias have interesting branching habits and can be used to create stunning arrangements. Do include some of the miniature Rex types; under glass they are just about the most colorful foliage plant you can find. An asterisk indicates plants for covered gardens.

*B. aridicaulis—tiny green leaves, white flowers.

B. boweri—green leaves with black-stitched edges.

B. 'Chance'—mottled leaves, pink flowers.

B. 'China Boy'—bright-green leaves, red stems and pink blooms.

B. dregei—bronze-red maple leaves, branching habit.

*B. griffithi—heart-shaped iridescent leaves.

*B. hydrocotylifolia—round dark-green leaves.

B. 'Lulandi'—bright-green leaves, pink flowers.

*B. 'Red Berry'—wine-red Rex type.

*B. 'Red Wing'—wine-red, silver edges on leaves; Rex type.

B. 'Rosa Kugel'—small green leaves; wax begonia.

B. rotundifolia—apple-green leaves, pink blooms.

B. 'Star Bright'—silver-and-green foliage; Red type.

B. 'Winter Jewel'—frosty green leaves, white blooms.

MINIATURE AFRICAN VIOLETS (SAINTPAULIA)

These popular plants need no introduction. With colorful flowers and handsome foliage, they are proven plants for covered or bubble glass gardens. In the first few weeks they may lose a few leaves; this is part of the adjustment to new conditions. Of prime importance for all plants—but especially for violets—is the soil. Use a loose, spongy, humusy mixture that is porous, while retaining moisture, so roots can breathe and excess water can drain through the soil. My mix is two parts garden soil to one part each of peat moss, charcoal, sand and leaf mold.

African violets are thought of as shade plants, but please, don't put them in darkness. They need light; a west exposure is fine. Give them warmth (78° F.) and ample humidity, say 60 to 70 percent. Watch gardens for signs of mildew or botrytis, seen as gray mold on the plants. Allow some air to circulate in the container during the day—take off the cover for an hour or two or put matchsticks under the rim of the dome to allow air to enter

51

the garden. If the disease is severe, dust plants with a fungicide (Captan or Zineb).

Try these varietals:

'Honeyette'—red-lavender.   'Tinkle'—lavender.

'Lavender Elfin Girl'—lavender.   'Tiny Bells'—dark blue.

'Minneapolis'—pink.   'Wendy'—blue.

'Pink Rock'—pink.

MINIATURE ORCHIDS

Only a few years ago, miniature orchids were rarely seen. Today there are thousands to choose from. These delightful gems are perfect for miniature glass gardens. Some, like restrepia and schlimii, need coolness and good air circulation to thrive, so they belong in open containers. Others like bulbophyllums and cirrhopetalums naturally grow in moist warm forests and need the protection of the closed garden.

These orchids come in 2- or 3-inch-diameter pots of fir bark or osmunda, or on slabs of tree fern. When you put them into the arrangement try to use the same potting material. Prepare the drainage bed and then crack the pots the orchids are in; most times, the root ball will stay in place. Put the ball of roots into a pocket of soil and camouflage the surface with sphagnum moss. Or, if on slabs of tree fern, simply arrange the miniature orchids in the garden utilizing the tree fern as part of the arrangement. There are orchids for shade, others for sun; some need warmth and others require coolness.

At the start, do not water the plants too much; keep them quite dry until the crucial adjustment period is over; this is about six weeks. Mist them frequently.

The following miniatures are some of my favorites. An asterisk indicates plants for covered gardens.

Angraecum compactum—a stunning 5-inch orchid with large fragrant white flowers. Give some sun, warmth (70° F. at night). *A. falcatum*, with smaller flowers, grows to 6 inches; needs some sun.

Ascocentrum ampullaceum—to 8 inches with erect scapes of brilliant red flowers; needs some sun. Dependable.

Broughtonia sanguinea—to 4 inches with panicles of bright-red flowers. Needs sun.

Bulbophyllum—a large genus with some delightful miniatures: *B. barbigerum*—intricate flower with purple-brown hairs; *B. lemniscatoides*—an oddity of nature with small dark-purplish flowers; *B. morphologorum*—another unusual orchid with hundreds of small yellow-brown flowers to a head. Grow all species in sunny glass garden.

Capanemia uliginosa—to 4 inches with lovely scented flowers. Give sun.

Cirrhopetalum—a large group of orchids with many splendid miniatures. Try: *C. Cumingii*—red and pink flowers in a half-circle design; *C. Roxburghii*—an umbrella of tiny pink flowers. Give scattered sun.

Gastrochilus bellinus—to 6 inches with leathery green foliage and fragrant yellow flowers. Scattered sun.

Leptotes bicolor—to 5 inches with a 3-inch white flower stained magenta. Sun or shade.

Masdevallia—a fine genus of unusual orchids with many small species. All require coolness (60° F. at night) and partial shade. Try: *M. bella*—triangular yellow flower spotted red: *M. horrida*—only 2 inches tall, with greenish-yellow flowers dotted red; *M. infracta*—to 6 inches with purple blooms.

Ornithocephalus bicornis—to 3 inches with whitish-green flowers. Needs sun.

Restrepia elegans—to 2 inches with fantastic yellow flowers dotted with red. Needs coolness and shade.

Stelis guatemalenis—to 8 inches with diminutive greenish-white flowers. Grow cool (58° F. at night) in shade.

JEWEL ORCHIDS

These orchids are grown for their foliage and not their flowers. And the foliage is unique in the plant world. Leaf coloring is dark brown, maroon, green-black, with silver or bronze veins or sometimes reticulated with finely etched white lines.

Only recently have these plants appeared in catalogues, and because they are so unusual you may want to try a few. They need high humidity and warmth (never less than 78° F.). I have grown the species listed here in a dome garden and they have responded beautifully—unlike those I tried to grow many years ago as windowsill plants, which died within a month.

Give them a rich planting mix—one-third soil, one-third shredded osmunda and one-third perlite or other porous stone. Keep them shaded.

Anoectochilus Roxburghii—to 6 inches, velvety-green leaves veined with gold lines.
Erythroides nobilis argyrocentrus—to 8 inches, gray-green leaves with silver lines.

Haemeria discolor 'Dawsoniana'—to 8 inches, dark, velvety reddish-green leaves laced with copper red.

Haemeria nigricans—velvety, almost black foliage.

CACTI AND SUCCULENTS

With some 1,300 species distributed among 200 genera, the cactus family is huge. There are hundreds of charming minia-

Many cacti will grow well in sandy soil and a wide-mouthed glass container.

tures to grow. While most cacti are succulents, not all succulents are cacti. Cacti store water in their thickened stems, which eliminates the need for leaves. Succulents, on the other hand, use their fleshy leaves as water reservoirs. Because there are so many kinds to choose from, make selections carefully. Search for the interesting species, the ones with unusual shape or other attractive features—and while bloom may not be heavy in the glass garden, the plants stay small for years and need little attention.

Many of the succulents, and especially the cacti, must be grown almost dry in winter. Use a sandy soil for both types. In summer, keep the soil evenly moist. Desert landscapes are popular because they can live for years with almost no care—only an occasional watering. These plants are not for the covered garden; they need sun and free air circulation and so they must be planted in a wide-mouthed glass container.

Aloe variegata—a rosette of green-and-white leaves.

Astrophytum myriostigma (bishop's-cap)—spineless species shaped like a bishop's cap.

Cephalocereus senilis (old man cactus)—white wooly hair; grows slowly, and a real oddity.

55

Cotyledon teretifolia—clusters of erect, dark-green hairy leaves; pale-yellow flowers in summer.

Crassula—a large group with many small plants: *C. cooperi*— pointed leaves with black blotches; *C. schmidtii*—dwarf rosette of pink leaves. Others to try are *C. falcata* and *C. argentea* (jade plant).

Echeveria derenbergii (painted lady)—pale-green leaves tipped bright red.

Echinocereus dasyacathus—a short-spined, easily grown species; large yellow flowers.

Echinopsis multiplex—dark-green close-ribbed barrel with sharp brown spines.

Euphorbia 'Bojeri'—dwarf crown of thorns, with dark-green tiny leaves and brilliant red bracts.

Faucaria tigrina (tiger jaw)—handsome gray-green plant spotted with white; yellow flowers.

Gasteria lilliputana—spirally arranged, thick, short stubby dark-green leaves mottled with pale green.

Gymnocalycium mihanovichii (chin cactus)—attractive small plant with banded ribs.

Haworthia fasciata (zebra haworthia)—dark-green leaves banded crosswise with rows of white dots.

Kalanchoe—many fine small plants in this group: *K. Blossfeld-iana*—fresh green leaves and red flowers; many varieties; *K. pumila*—frosted green leaves and plum-colored flowers; *K. To-mentosa*—fat leaves covered with felt.

Kleinia repens (blue chalk stick)—brilliant blue-green cylindrical leaves.

Mammillaria bocasana (powderpuff cactus)—globular, with soft, fluffy white hair, creamy flowers.

56

Notocactus ottonis (Indian head)—small glossy green globe with short needlelike spines.

Opuntia microdasya (bunny ears)—short spineless pads brushed with golden tufts.

Rebutia minuscula (crown cactus)—small globe with fiery red flowers.

Sedum—large group with some excellent small species: *S. adolphii* —rosettes of yellow green; *S. multiceps*—dark-green branched plant; and *S. jepsonii*—fleshy purple leaves.

DWARF TREES

Seedling trees are especially handsome when grown under glass. They give meaning to plant groups, help to define an area to make it seem like a real living landscape. While there are stunted trees and grafted trees, I leave these to the experts in bonsai. I have experimented with seedling trees and dwarf varieties. These are naturally slow-growing and come in many shapes—conical, columnar, globular, pyramidal, weeping—and range in color from pale gold to red, from blue-green to silver. Most of them endure a shallow base of soil and enjoy the humid atmosphere of a covered container. And it takes them several years to outgrow a miniature garden.

You can easily root cuttings of American yew or juniper. Spruce, balsam, fir and white pine can be used too, but take them when they are very young. Arborvitae does well but needs a large container. You can buy some dwarf varieties at nurseries or from mail-order specialists.

Keep plants in a bright garden and in an unheated but not freezing place. Even a single specimen under a glass dome attracts attention.

Here are some dwarf species I have used for glass gardens:

Abies balsamea nana (fir)—nice globe-shaped evergreen.

Chamaecyparis obtusa compacta—compact form, glossy green. Branching.

Chamaecyparis obtusa nana aurea (cypress)—dense globe of golden needles.

Juniperus communis compressa—slender columnar shape.

Juniperus procumbens nana—dark-green creeper.

Picea abies nana (spruce)—dwarf form of Norway spruce; dense branches, short needles.

Taxus cuspidata nana (yew)—dark evergreen leaves; red berry fruit.

Thuja minima (arborvitae)—a slow-growing ball.

Thuja pumila 'Little Gem'—globe-shaped, with dense growth.

Tsuga canadensis compacta (hemlock)—dense, slow-growing, glossy green globe.

PESTS AND DISEASES

You are not likely to need insecticides when you garden in glass. Small plants have small problems, and a mammoth infestation of insects rarely happens. Keep an aerosol can of a general insecticide on hand for aphids and mealybugs, and a good fungicide to help you clean up fungus if it develops. Of course, the best prevention is inspecting new arrivals carefully before setting them in place and taking immediate steps at the first sign of disease or infestation. Too, sterile soil goes a long way in keeping the garden free of pests.

Sometimes, even with the best care, plants do become infected. Here is a list to help you recognize the symptoms, know the ailment, and suggest the treatment to cure it.

Pests

Insect	What to Look For	Where to Look	Treatment
Aphids	Colored oval insects	On new leaves and in stem axils	Spray with Malathion
Mealybugs	White cottony insects	Undersides of leaves, on stems	Spray with Malathion
Red Spider Mites	Too small to be seen; look for webs	Leaf axils	Apply Dimite
Scale	Hard brown or green insects	On leaves, at base of plant	Scrape off with toothpick or apply nicotine sulphate
Slugs	Slimy shell-less snails	Hide in soil or under pots	Apply Buggeta to soil, under pots
Thrips	Small sucking insects	On leaves	Spray with Malathion
White Flies	Tiny winged insects	On leaves, soil	Spray with Malathion

Diseases

Plants in bottle garden and covered gardens are occasionally victims of a fungus disease, a gray mold that lives on dead and decaying flowers and leaves. If detected promptly, there is little danger of losing plants to the disease. The cure is simple. Remove affected parts, let more air into the garden, provide bright light and avoid excessive heat. After cutting away affected areas of the plant, it is a good idea to dust the plant with a fungicide (Captan or Zineb).

Mildew is a bacterial disease that occurs in plants kept in a confined space. It appears as a grayish-white powdery film on leaves or stems. Remove the affected parts and dust the plant with a fungicide.

In covered gardens, check glass surfaces frequently for too much condensation and watch plants for minute beads of moisture on the leaves. Pretty as this may be, it indicates there is too much moisture in the garden. Lifting the cover a fraction of an inch until the condition disappears will help eliminate the possibility of mildew or fungus problems.

5 · Plants for Special Gardens

SOME PLANTS enjoy the warmth and humidity of a covered garden—a stoppered bottle or decanter, a dome garden, a jar with a lid. Other plants need the conditions of a partially open garden—a bubble bowl, a brandy snifter or an aquarium —where there is less moisture.

It is important to put the right plants in the right kind of container to assure them proper growing conditions. Desert-type cacti and succulents will not live long in a covered garden and moisture-loving orchids and ferns simply will not do well in a partially open garden. There are so many miniature plants and seedlings to choose from that it is easy to find the right plant for the right container.

Select plants carefully and arrange them attractively to create a living picture that will give you satisfaction as it grows and changes over the years.

PLANTS FOR COVERED CONTAINERS

Acorus gramineus pusillus—tufts of iris-like leaves to 4 inches; compact sculptural foliage. Good in corners or near but not touching the glass in groups of two or three plants.

Adiantum hispidulum—one of the many useful ferns with dark-green branching fronds.

60

Allophytum mexicanum—fine flowering plant with dark-green oval leaves and lavender blooms. Grows to 5 inches.

Alternantha versicolor—pink, green, and white wrinkled foliage; nice color for garden. To about 7 inches.

Begonia—large family with some stellar miniatures (see Chapter 4).

Caladium—striking plants with variegated leaves; many varieties. Good accent.

Calathea argyraea—low and compact with blotched green leaves lined with silver. *C. rosea picta* also good, with variegated foliage. Both plants grow to about 8 inches.

Cissus striata (miniature grape ivy)—a lacy climber with scalloped leaves; hard to beat in a closed garden.

Dionea muscipula (Venus fly trap)—popular carnivorous plant that flourishes in a closed garden; does not need flies to eat to survive.

Erythroides nobilis argynoneurus—one of the charming jewel orchids; leaves are gray-green etched with silver. Expensive, but outstanding in the garden.

Fittonia verschaffeltii (mosaic plant)—velvety green leaves laced with veins of contrasting color. One of my favorites. *F. argyroneura* has green leaves with white veins; also nice.

Haemeria discolor 'Dawsoniana'—the popular jewel orchid with dark, velvety reddish-green foliage. Must be seen to be believed.

Hedera helix species—ivy is always appealing in the closed garden, especially the wavy-edged crinkly varieties. Many to choose from. See growers' catalogues.

Malpighia coccigera (miniature holly)—small glossy leaves; whitish-pink flowers. Tends to be straggly, so prune occasionally.

Maranta tricolor—exotic multicolored oval leaves.

Orchids—see Chapter 4.

A pedestal bowl and a graceful dome set off this contrasting foliage.

Pellaea rotundifolia (button fern)—dark-green round leaves on wiry stems. Highly recommended.

Pellionia Daveauana—handsome leaves edged in chocolate brown.

Peperomia—large group of many miniatures, one prettier than the other. Good fill-in material.

Pilea—a genus with many creepers; branching stems and colored and patterned foliage. Excellent are: *P. nummularifolia, P. mi-*

62

crophylla, P. depressa. Use with caution because they tend to go rampant. Upright growers include: *P.* 'Silver Tree,' *P. cadierei minima* and *P. repens.*

Polystichum tsus simense—an 8-inch dwarf fern with leathery dark-green fronds; a capable performer.

Pteris ensiformis '*Victoriae*'—showy silver and dark-green foliage; tidy habit.

Rosa—miniature varieties increase in popularity daily; tiny delightful replicas of large roses. See Chapter 4.

Saintpaulia—African violet; many delightful miniatures; stellar plants. See Chapter 4.

Saxifraga sarmentosa (strawberry geranium)—a favorite, with rosettes of round silver-veined leaves; many varieties and all good.

Selaginella Kraussiana Brownii—a true creeper with grass-green foliage, and foolproof in a closed garden. *S. uncinata*, with blue-green leaves, is also good.

Siderasis fuscata—velvety brownish-red leaves.

Sinningia pusilla (miniature gloxinia)—a true gem with soft round leaves and pale-lavender flowers. Not to be missed; many new varieties.

Tradescantia multiflora (inch plant)—creeping dark-green foliage. Use with caution; can take over a small garden.

PLANTS FOR PARTIALLY OPEN CONTAINERS

Abutilon hybrids (flowering maple)—soft gray-green leaves and paper-thin bell-shaped flowers make these appealing plants. Young plants bloom readily; many varieties.

Achimenes—large group of charming performers with velvet-soft leaves and tubular flowers. Search for small varieties.

Adromischus—miniature succulents; many kinds and all good in the open garden.

Aglaonema pictum—outstanding foliage species with blue-green leaves splashed with silver.

Aloe brevifolia—a member of the lily family with sharp spiny leaves; nice sculptural quality. Has striped leaves and is good accent plant.

Carissa grandiflora 'Boxwood Beauty'—dwarf; a fine tropical evergreen with glossy leaves and white flowers.

Crassula—a varied group of succulents with many miniatures; some are ill-shaped, so choose carefully. I recommend: *C. Cooperi*—tufts of pointed leaves, occasionally pale-pink flowers, *C. schmidtii*—handsome, with pointed pinkish leaves, pink blooms.

Cryptanthus—a group of bromeliads also called "earth stars" or "rainbow plants." Decorative and appealing, they need almost no care. Try these for real satisfaction: *C. bivittatus* (*roseus picta*)—salmon-rose striped foliage; *C. bromelioides tricolor*—multicolored foliage; and *C. zonatus*—zebra bands of silver and green.

Cyanotis somaliensis (pussy ears)—bright-green leaves edged with white fuzz resembling pussy ears.

Dyckia fosteriana—a bromeliad with silver-spined leaves.

Echeveria derenbergii—green leaves margined red, with orange flowers.

Euphorbia 'Bojeri' (dwarf crown of thorns)—a truly lovely plant with tiny dark-green leaves and vivid red bracts. Good accent.

Faucaria—low succulents with triangular gray-green leaves; attractive and carefree. Try: *F. tigrina* (tiger jaw) with yellow flowers, or *F. tuberculosa*.

Haworthia—small succulents with ribbed leaves. *H. fasciata* has striped foliage and *H. margaritifera* bears dark-green foliage with white dots.

This well-planned bubble garden includes pilea, peperomia, aucuba, dizygotheca and ivy.

Osmanthus fragrans (sweet olive)—hardly a miniature, but young plants can be grown successfully. Desirable because of lovely scent.

Oxalis—tropicals with buttercup-like flowers. Only a few are small; others generally too large for miniature garden. Try: *O. hedysaroides rubra* with rich butter-yellow flowers and *O. henrei* (*herrerae*) with tiny yellow blooms.

65

Pelargonium (Geranium)—many fine miniatures. See Chapter 4.

Rebutia minuscula (crown cactus)—an amenable cactus and one of the few that produces its fiery red flowers in the home.

Saintpaulia—popular African violets; many delightful miniatures. See Chapter 4.

Tillandsia ionanthe—a tiny bromeliad that bears violet flowers in spring.

PLANTS FOR THEME GARDENS

Selecting a theme for the garden makes it easy to create a harmonious, pleasing arrangement. While there are many different kinds of gardens—rustic, informal, formal and so on— the tropical, woodland and Oriental settings are most popular. Theme gardens can be planted in small containers, but for a stunning effect a somewhat large housing—an aquarium or five-gallon water bottle or 16-inch-diameter goldfish bowl—is necessary.

Tropical theme

Here is where you can have all kinds of small tropical plants to create a lush effect; while you do not want the scene to be crowded, you do want many plants. Use creeping ground-cover and miniature ferns, orchids and bromeliads. The terrain should be hilly rather than flat, and this garden is better-looking without props or figurines. Give it bright light and a standard soil for plants, except the orchids and bromeliads (they need pockets of osmunda or fir bark). Or leave them in the tiny pots they come in and sink pot and all into the soil. But crack the pots first and then settle them into position.

66

Among plants that can be used for a tropical theme are:

Bambusa nana—dwarf bamboo; fresh green leaves. Graceful.

Carissa grandiflora 'Boxwood Beauty'—tropical evergreen; dwarf. Thick glossy green leaves. Prune to desired shape.

Euonymous japonicus microphyllus—bright-green leaves with pale-yellow veins.

Ficus pumila minima (creeping fig)—miniature; heart-shaped dark-green leaves.

Fragaria indica—a trailer that looks good against the glass. Occasionally bears yellow flowers.

Malpighia coccigera (miniature holly)—tiny bright-green hollylike foliage.

Punica granatum nana—dwarf pomegranate; bright-green leaves and red fruit.

These plants for a tropical theme require a cool temperature—54°F. to 62°F.—at night.

Cyclamen neapolitanum—dark-green leaves with silver markings. Fine rose-colored flowers.

Exacum affine—blue flowers.

Miniature geraniums—all colors; all kinds of foliage. See Chapter 4.

Saxifraga sarmentosa (strawberry geranium)—glossy dark-green foliage; a popular, robust plant.

Streptocarpus saxorum—round leaves and funnel-shaped blue flowers.

Woodland Theme

This is a popular setting, always fresh and inviting and cheerful, especially on gray winter mornings. Put in a few stepping-stones and some interesting rocks. Here is where you can be somewhat quaint in your selections. Use a rather large glass container. Average living-room temperatures and 50 percent humidity with about three hours of sun will make these plants thrive in the woodland setting.

Acorus gramineus variegata—grassy leaves; a pretty, tiny plant, ideal for glass gardens.

Azalea 'Gumpo'—tiny, with bright-red flowers.

Begonia 'China Doll'—light-green leaves with purple markings.

Begonia 'Medora'—small glossy green leaves.

Ficus diversiloba (mistletoe fig)—dark-green leaves with brown spots.

Hedera helix 'Glacier'—variegated triangular ivy leaves.

Kalanchoe 'Tom Thumb'—bright-red flowers for Christmas.

Oxalis hedysaroides rubra—burgundy leaves; yellow flowers.

Pellaea rotundifolia (button fern)—stellar fern with buttonlike leaves.

Selaginella Kraussiana—creeping mosslike plant that makes an excellent groundcover.

Sinningia pusilla—miniature gloxinia with slipper-shaped lavender flowers veined with violet. One of the best.

Oriental Theme

Simplicity is the keynote of this garden, but many times what seems simple is really quite difficult to achieve. The very nature of the theme—sparse beauty—means that just one feature out of proportion to the whole will ruin the setting. Stones, mosses and figurines must be selected with care. Use only a few plants and leave space for a path. Use marble chips (and some charcoal granules for contrast) for surface paving. For trees,

A small rock and a fuzzy-leaved saxifraga *make an interesting combination in this graceful bowl garden.*

select an upright plant with a single stem and a bent or twisted shape. Grow a few strands of grass that look like bamboo. Choose a suitable container; a three-legged clay saucer about 12 inches in diameter is simple, handsome and in keeping with the theme; or select a pedestal dish. Raising the scene off the ground gives it more appeal.

Acorus gramineus variegatus—grassy, tiny and graceful.

Begonia dreigei—small bronze-red maple-shaped leaves.

Gasteria lilliputana—thick short, sturdy dark-green leaves mottled with pale green.

69

Laelia pumila—miniature orchid with large rose-colored blooms.

Punica granatum nana—good accent tree for Oriental garden.

Sedum multiceps—dark gray-green needlelike leaves.

Tillandsia ionanthe—miniature bromeliad with violet flowers.

HERB GARDENS

Apothecary or candy jars are good containers for growing herbs. Be sure jars have wide necks so it will be easy to harvest the herbs. Prepare the planting bed the same way as for other gardens, with drainage material, including some charcoal granules, peat moss and compost. Keep the soil evenly moist and firm. Sow seeds—thyme, chives, parsley—sparingly. Cover the jar with the lid and place in a bright, warm (76° F.) place. When seeds have germinated, thin them out ruthlessly; leave only the strongest seedlings and dispose of the weaklings. There will not be space in the jar for more than three or four mature plants. As the seedlings grow, turn the jar occasionally so all of them can get light.

You will find these herb gardens decorative on a sunny window in the kitchen, and useful as well, when you snip off a few green pieces from a growing plant for a salad or seasoning.

Basil—only 2 inches high; white or purplish flowers.

Chervil—fine fernlike leaves; white blooms.

Chive—grasslike leaves, lavender flowers. Good substitute for onion.

Parsley—dark-green tightly curled leaves.

Thyme—small green leaves, tiny lavender flowers.

6 · Woodland Plants

ONE OF THE ADVANTAGES of miniature glass gardening is that plants can be grown that do not survive in average home conditions. Woodland plants that we see only in the forest—if we have a chance to visit the forest at all—thrive in the protection of a glass container. Club moss, selaginellas and native ferns are seldom seen outside their native habitat, and yet they are intensely interesting when viewed close up. With careful handling, they can be as lovely in a glass garden as they are in the woods. Bog plants and wildflowers are other possibilities, but please do not rip them from forest floors. In most areas, this is prohibited by law, and further, most of these species are extremely difficult to cultivate. However, if by some chance you know an area that is going to be bulldozed for future building, get permission from the property owner to save the wildflowers from the wrecking crew.

Now many woodland plants can be ordered from mail-order specialists and occasionally from local nurseries. And pot-grown species are easier to transplant and grow than native plants. Of the native woodland subjects, ferns, mosses and selaginellas offer the best chance of survival in a glass garden.

The soil is the most vital part of growing woodland plants successfully in containers. It should be rich in leaf mold and be able to hold many times its weight in moisture. I use one-third part of leaf mold, one-third humus and one-third porous stones.

71

For bog-garden plants, I use equal parts of leaf mold and humus.

Most woodland plants can be bought inexpensively from mail-order specialists. They arrive in sphagnum moss, each species properly labeled; I try to get them into the glass garden the day they arrive. If you have permission to dig woodland plants, or where they are not protected by law, dig deep and take as much of the surrounding soil as you can. This helps to protect the roots, and when you transplant, the shock will not be so severe. Keep the plants in moist sphagnum moss until you get them home.

While woodland plants generally prefer a cool shady place, remember that in the woods, in early spring, leafless trees allow a good deal of light to filter through to the ground. Do not grow plants in total darkness; give them some light. I find a west window perfect for gardens with woodland plants. And remember that if you want to grow carnivorous species, they will need some sun daily.

SELAGINELLAS

Sometimes called moss ferns, selaginellas are botanically neither mosses nor ferns but fall somewhere between. They are charming nonflowering plants in many shades of green. Some need warmth and humidity; the majority thrive in coolness in a moist shady setting. There are many small creeping species as well as some upright growers.

Here are the species I usually work with:

S. denticulata—a rampant creeper that needs space.

S. emmeliana—small, light-green lacy foliage.

S. hepatica—larger plant, tends to ramble.

S. uncinata—feathery and attractive; grows quickly.

72

MOSSES (LYCOPODIUMS)

Mosses are not very pretty when they appear in lawns or pot plants. But grown with ferns, and when examined closely, they are truly beautiful. Mosses generally are classified as bog, woodland or rock mosses. However, rock mosses grow on earth as well as on stone, and woodland mosses grow on trees or earth. The yellow-green and olive-green mosses clinging to earth are best for the miniature covered garden.

Without protection mosses dry out quickly and shrivel in a dry atmosphere, but in the confines of a humid case they are an interesting nature study. Many different species can be found on tree roots, decaying tree stumps, in fields, on old walls and shady lanes. You can spot them as brilliant patches of green made up of many minute plants.

Here are some mosses for the covered case:

L. clavatum—4-inch stems with needlelike leaves.

L. lucidulum—dark-green foliage.

L. obscurum—about 6 inches, charming.

FERNS

The fern family is large and varied, and while we are familiar with Boston ferns and bird's-nest ferns as house plants, woodland ferns are seldom seen in the home. In covered gardens, where it is cool, shady, and moist, these plants will charm you. They cannot be beat for their decorative appeal. Most of them are lacy in lovely shades of green, fresh and crisp.

Ferns are found growing in woods, bogs, marshes and mountains, generally in partial shade. A few exceptions like Asplenium trichomanes and A. ruta-muraria need dry hot conditions but these, too, will adjust to covered gardens.

To grow ferns from spores—the funny seedlike bodies on the back of the fronds—shake the dustlike spores onto a mix of equal parts sand and peat moss. Use shallow pans, and cover with a dome. Give the seeds heat (76° F.) and even moisture. In about a year (depending on the plant being grown) the tiny plants can be put into 2-inch-diameter pots and set in a warm shady place in the glass garden.

The following ferns are usually available from suppliers:

Adiantum—many varieties of this beautiful fern; use small seedlings. Generally dormant in winter, these plants may grow all year in a case. *A. cuneatum gracillum*—delicate lacy fronds; *A. pedatum*—graceful curved fronds.

Asplenium—ideal plants for glass gardens; prefer shade and neutral soil. Easy to grow. *A. platyneuron* (ebony spleenwort)— about 12 inches tall; feathery fronds with brownish-purple stems; *A. trichomanes* (maidenhair spleenwort)—to 6 inches; thick clustered fronds with 1-inch leaflets on black ribs; *A. ruta-muraria* (wall rue)—to 4 inches; tough leathery dark-green fronds.

Belchnum—good ferns for a large case; these revel in saturated atmosphere and partial shade. Use young plants. Try *B. spicant* (hard fern)—dark glossy evergreen fronds; easy to grow.

Botrychium—found in open woods with moderate moisture; grows to about 20 inches. Young seedlings prosper in covered gardens. Try *B. virginianum* (rattlesnake fern).

Camptosorus rhyzophyllus (walking fern)—diminutive charmer with small evergreen fronds. Plants root at the tips and "walk" over the soil.

Cyrtomium (holly fern)—sturdy and shiny, with stiff fronds.

Dryopteris—grows in damp places; dark-green plants, variable in size. *D. cristata*—evergreen blue-green fronds; *D. Linnaeaena* (oak fern), sometimes classified as *Polypodium dryopteris*.

Above: A garden in a brandy snifter in various stages of preparation. This is an easy type for the beginner to plant. Opposite: The finished garden— a lovely gift or a colorful decorative note for any room in the house.

Pellaea rotundifolia (button fern)—blue-green fronds with rolled edges and fuzzy brown root stock in a globular mass. Does not like temperature changes.

Polypodium—group of handsome ferns that thrive in shade and moisture. Easy to grow; charming. Try: *P. vulgare* (common polypody)—evergreen fronds, to about 8 inches. Likes coolness.

Polystichum—shade-loving group; very decorative. *P. setiferum* (hedge fern)—feathery fronds covered with brown hairlike scales.

Pteris—delightful wee ferns; several kinds. Ideal glass-case plants and vigorous growers. *P. cretica* (ribbon fern)—delicate fronds to about 6 inches; *P. ensiformis evergemiensis*—silver-and-green fronds.

76

BOG PLANTS

Bog gardens may not sound very attractive, but partridge berry, goldthread and bunchberry stay fresh, green and lovely for many months in a container. Bog plants need sphagnum moss and much moisture, and they do not want to be too crowded or in excessive heat. The bog habitat needs a large glass case and, if possible, a watery corner for water plants. The trick with bog gardens is to provide them with extreme coolness during dusk.

Here are some plants for the bog garden:

Chimaphila maculata (striped pipsissewa)—handsome variegated foliage.

Chimaphila umbellata (common pipsissewa)—leaves that resemble the groundcover pachysandra.

Chiogenes hispidula (snowberry)—shiny leaves on a creeping vine. Fragrant; must have coolness.

Coptis trifolia (goldthread)—4 inches tall, with cloverlike leaves and waxy white flowers.

Epigea repens (trailing arbutus)—a longtime favorite; a cheerful creeper with woody, hairy stems and green leaves. Delightful, fragrant bellshaped flowers.

Goodyera pubescens (rattlesnake plantain)—woodland orchid with curiously marked leaves.

Hepatica Americana—maroon-tinted foliage.

Mitchella repens (partridge berry)—red berries, grassy-green leaves make this a stellar plant.

Pyrola elliptica (shinleaf or wintergreen)—oval green leaves. Does not like as much moisture as other bog plants.

78

A refrigerator jar makes a handsome container. PHOTO: JOYCE R. WILSON

CARNIVOROUS PLANTS

Don't let the heading scare you; these are utterly charming plants with lovely flowers and handsome foliage. They deserve more popularity than they have, but they are difficult to grow in the average home. However, they flourish in glass containers

79

where they have high humidity and ample moisture. Most of them are small, ideal for the closed case.

These oddities, among which are the cobra plants, Venus flytraps and pitcher plants, live on a diet of insects attracted to their odor. Once ensnared, the insect is digested by the plant by means of internal chemical fluids. The digested nutrients are absorbed by the plant tissue. But if your home is not an insect haven, do not think the plants will starve. They do not need insects or raw meat to survive.

Use a planting bed of equal parts crushed charcoal, tiny stones and rich soil. Put a 2-inch basket of sphagnum moss over this. Place the garden where it will get some afternoon sun, and be sure the soil is always slightly damp.

These are the species I have successfully grown in glass containers:

Darlingtonia Californica (cobra plant)—handsome beige-and-red hooded stalks.

Dionea muscipula—the popular Venus fly trap; only 4 inches tall with bright-green wedge-shaped leaves with fine hairs along their edges.

Drosera rotundifolia—reddish-green leaves and fanciful white flowers. Only 2 inches tall.

Saracenia flava (Huntsman's horn)—exotic tubular blooms that resemble pitchers. Lovely, tall growers. Use young plants.

Saracenia purpurea (pitcher plant)—broadly winged pitcher, blooms beautifully veined red.

7 · The Vivarium: Tiny Creatures in a Glass Garden

CORRECTLY CALLED a vivarium, a case with living plants and small animals offers great nature study and hours of fascination. The small creatures make the glass garden come to life, a truly separate world that demands attention. A covered garden with plants can be a home for many different tiny critters— salamanders, lizards, chameleons, geckos. For the most part, these animals will care for themselves and become interesting pets.

HOW TO ASSEMBLE A VIVARIUM

While any odd-shaped glass container can be used for a vivarium, an aquarium is generally preferred. These are readily available in many sizes—five-gallon, 10-gallon, and so on. The tanks have sufficient air space and permit an undistorted scene of plants and animals. Whether you call it a terrarium or a vivarium, it is a piece of nature generally enclosed in glass and provides a natural environment for small creatures.

Decide what kind of scene you want. The desert setting is dry and sunny; the bog scene, wet and humid; and the woodlands

somewhere between the two. Then select the plants and animals that will thrive in the conditions the terrarium offers.

Start with a clean container and place gravel or bits of broken flower pots on the bottom and cover with fine sand to a 2-inch depth. Scatter some charcoal granules over the drainage material and add appropriate soil for the scene you are creating. Build up soil in places; make hills and valleys for interest. For a small pond for animals, sink a glass dish into the soil and edge it with tiny stones. Select your plants and place them so they have room to grow.

When the garden is planted, wet the soil but do not saturate it. Put the animals in the terrarium and cover it with a pane of glass to keep pets in and enemies out. The cover should allow some air to circulate in the garden. Except for the desert scene, which needs sun and warmth, other gardens require semishade and coolness.

Gardens with small animals need covers. Open-wire mesh (at hardware stores) is one answer. Simply bend the wire to the shape of the container and set it in place with a binding tape. Glass covers, of course, are the other answer. Glass looks better, and a local glass store will cut any shape or size for your vivarium. The cover should allow some air to circulate in the garden but do not leave enough gap on top to allow the small creatures to escape.

LIVESTOCK

Small tree frogs or chameleons can be trained to eat from your fingers or to wait on a leaf for their food. Even a few ladybugs in a miniature garden are fun to watch. Praying mantises or a colony of ants are interesting too as they go about their daily chores. Turtles, while popular with youngsters, have a hearty appetite and can strip the garden. For these use a sparse· planting arrangement and provide lettuce and watercress for food.

83

Opposite: A snail has settled comfortably in this native woodland garden.
PHOTO: ROCHE

Salamanders, with dark-blue skin dotted with light blue, need a moist terrain. Set a few pieces of decayed bark or some small stones in the garden. They love to hide but will generally come out to sun themselves. Salamanders prefer the moist buoyant atmosphere of the bog garden where there are some decayed branches or twigs they can hide under.

Chameleons are my favorites; they bound about the garden, will drink water from a medicine dropper and are a constant source of amusement. Unlike salamanders, which like to crawl under objects, chameleons like to climb. They enjoy a diet of honey, sweetened water, bits of ripe bananas and grains of sugar. Do not try to make them eat. Many of them can get along for several days without any food. Their color changes when they are excited, and generally it matches the rocks or plants upon which they lodge. These tiny clowns do not want to be in a very moist garden but are quite at home in the wood-land setting, where there is a moderate amount of moisture and where they can climb shrubby small plants. They are extremely graceful, distribute their weight evenly and do not harm the plants.

If you keep toads and frogs, be sure to provide them with a dish of water to soak in and mealworms (at pet stores) for food. You will need rather large glass gardens for toads and frogs; they like to roam and they do hide for days when they are hi-bernating. Generally, the woodland or bog garden suits them.

Geckos are attractive lizardlike animals with patterned skins of pinkish-beige and black. With large heads and long rounded pink tongues, these little fellows clamber all over a garden and have a great time. They do best in a desert setting with a few small succulents, rather than in the tropical garden. Set out a few small stones for them and have a section of clean dry sand in one area of the case.

Newts are small animals with tiny crocodile-like feet; they are inquisitive, colorful and at home in a bog garden. Other animals you might want to try are horned toads or some of the small lizards. Don't buy a sluggish animal; look for one that is alert and fast on its feet.

84

A salamander and a turtle share this vivarium.   PHOTO: JOYCE R. WILSON

The size of the case dictates what kind of animal to have. Certainly frogs will need more space then geckos. Do not put an animal in a tightly confined space. If you have only a brandy snifter, be content with an insect colony—ants or a few lady-bugs.

With all animals, remember to supply food and drink for them; this is your responsibility and just about all you have to do for them. Food is at local pet shops where you buy small animals.

In a glass container planted to represent their natural environment, creatures become more than curiosities. They are at home and can be watched as they conduct their daily lives. It is interesting to see the patterns of life they follow, just as we, in our daily living, do.

Watch your pets for signs of ill health. In most cases, the eyes indicate any trouble. A glassy or dull look signifies a sluggish or possibly an ailing animal.

GARDENS FOR YOUR PETS

Desert Gardens

Like the scaly or thick-skinned animals—lizards, gopher tortoise—that go into this garden, the plants too, are thick-skinned. In other words, they soak up water when it is available. Use a sandy gritty soil; build a mound in a corner so animals can sun themselves. Place a few stones or attractive twigs here to accent the area. Put the garden in warmth, where there is some sun during the day. If you don't have a sunny location for it, put one 60-watt incandescent light bulb above the terrarium for ten hours a day to simulate natural sun.

PLANTS	ANIMALS
Gasteria	Texas spiny lizard
Aloe	Fence lizard
Sedum	Horned toad or lizard
Astrophytum	Mediterranean gecko
Crassula	Gopher tortoise
Adromischus	

Woodland Gardens

Toads and chameleons enjoy the moist but not saturated atmosphere of the woodland scene. Here it is neither too warm nor too dry. There should be some sun, but not too much. Put in areas that offer some cover so animals can hide. Do not crowd the case with plants, and do maintain moderate temperatures and about 50 percent humidity. Use a soil containing chipped charcoal, sand and plenty of humus.

THE VIVARIUM: Tiny Creatures in a Glass Garden

PLANTS	ANIMALS
Philodendron	American chameleon
Orchids	Texas spiny lizard
Fittonia	Mediterranean gecko
Calathea	Eastern glass lizard
Maranta	Salamanders
Anthurium	Toads
	Turtles

Bog Gardens

The bog is damp; ferns and mosses thrive in it. So will non-aquatic newts and salamanders and wood turtles. The bog garden must be in a large container—never less than a ten-gallon tank. Use a humusy soil and place the garden in semishade and coolness (60°F. at night). Make small cliffs or hills to add interest to the terrain.

PLANTS	ANIMALS
Carnivorous species	Tree frogs
Mitchella (partridge berry)	Wood frogs
Chiogenes (creeping snowberry)	Toads
Asplenium platyneuron (ebony spleenwort)	Salamanders
Lycopodium (club mosses)	Newts
Polypodium vulgare (Polypody fern)	Mud turtles

WHERE TO BUY PLANTS

Alberts & Merkel Bros. Inc.
Box 537
Boynton Beach, Fla. 33435

Orchids and bromeliads.
Catalog 25¢

Allgrove, Arthur E.
279 Woburn Street
N. Wilmington, Mass. 01888

Native plants; carnivorous species.
Catalog 25¢

Beahm Gardens
2686 Pamoa Street
Pasadena, Calif. 91107

Cacti and succulents.
Catalog free

Buell's Greenhouses
Eastford, Conn. 06242

Miniature African violets.
Catalog 10¢

Burgess Seed & Plant Co.
67 E. Battle Creek Street
Galesburg, Mich. 49053

Seeds, plants, carnivorous species.
Catalog free

Burt's Nursery
P.O. Box 776
Jupiter, Fla. 33458

Bromeliads, tropical
plants

Cook's Geranium Nursery
712 N. Grand
Lyons, Kansas

Miniature geraniums.
Catalog 25¢

Craven's Greenhouses
4732 W. Tennessee
Denver, Colorado 80219

Miniature African violets

Fischer's Greenhouses
Dept. HC
Linwood, N.J. 08221

Miniature African violets,
gesneriads. Catalog 25¢

Hauserman's Orchids
Box 363
Elmhurst, Ill. 60128

Miniature orchids. Catalog free

Ilgenfritz, Margaret, Orchids
Monroe, Mich. 48161

Miniature orchids. Catalog 25¢

Johnson Cactus Gardens
Paramount, Calif. 90723

Cacti and succulents. Catalog 10¢

Kartuz Greenhouses
92 Chestnut Street
Wilmington, Mass. 01887

Miniature begonias, African
violets. Catalog 25¢

Leslie's Wildflower Nursery
30 Summer Street
Methuen, Mass. 01884

Wildflowers

Logee's Greenhouses
55 North Street
Danielson, Conn. 06239

Miniature begonias, geraniums.
Catalog 25¢

Lyon, Lyndon
14 Mutchler St.
Dolgeville, N.Y. 13329

Miniature African violets.
List free

Merry Gardens
Camden, Maine

Tropical plants. Catalog 25¢

Oakhurst Gardens
Box 444
Arcadia, Calif. 91008

Miniature orchids and bromeliads
Catalog 25¢

Park, George W., Co.
Greenwood, S.C. 29647

Seeds, plants. Catalog free

Robin, Clyde
P.O. Box 2091
Castro Valley, Calif. 94546

Wildflowers. Catalog 50¢

WHERE TO BUY PLANTS

Tinari Greenhouses
2325 Valley Rd.
Huntingdon Valley, Pa. 19006

Miniature African violets, gesneriads. Catalog free.

Tropical Paradise Greenhouses
8825 W. 79th Street
Overland Park, Kansas 66204

Tropical plants. Catalog 50¢

Wilson Bros.
Roachdale, Ind. 46172

Miniature geraniums. Catalog free.

WHERE TO BUY CONTAINERS, DOMES, TERRARIUMS

Allgrove, Arthur E.
279 Woburn Street
N. Wilmington, Mass. 01887

Glass cases, supplies; figurines

Crystal Glass Tube & Cylinder Co.
7310 S. Chicago Ave.
Chicago, Ill. 60619

Domes, cylinders

Owens-Illinois Glass Co.
Toledo, Ohio 43601

Glass containers of all kinds to the trade only. Products available at florist shops

Park, George W., Co.
Greenwood, S. C. 29647

Terrariums

A. L. Randall Co.
1325 Randolph St.
Chicago, Ill.

Glass containers of all kinds to the trade only. Products available at florist shops

West Virginia Glass Specialty Co.
Weston, W. Va. 26452

Glass containers of all kinds to the trade only. Available at florist shops

SUGGESTED READING

Ashberry, Anne, *Bottle Gardens and Fern Cases*. London, Hodder and Stoughton Ltd., 1964.

Brilmayer, Bernice, *All About Miniature Plants and Gardens*. Garden City, New York, Doubleday & Co., 1963.

Chidamian, Claude, *Cacti and Other Succulents*. Garden City, New York, Doubleday & Co., 1955.

Free, Montague, *All About House Plants*. Garden City, New York, Doubleday & Co., 1946.

Genders, Roy, *Gardening in Miniature*. London, Robert Hale Ltd., 1958.

Graf, Albert Byrd, *Exotica III*. Rutherford, New Jersey, Julius Roehrs, 1966.

Kramer, Jack, *Rare Orchids Everyone Can Grow*. Garden City, New York, Doubleday & Co., 1968.

McDonald, Elvin, *Miniature Plants*. Princeton, New Jersey, D. Van Nostrand Co., Inc., 1962.

Wilson, Helen Van Pelt, *The Joy of Geraniums*. New York, M. Barrows & Co., 1967.

PAMPHLETS AND PERIODICALS

Audubon Nature Bulletin, Series 4, Number 1, *The Terrarium*.

Audubon Nature Bulletin, Series 16, Number 8, *Adventures with Wild Plants, Indoors and Out*.

Brooklyn Botanic Gardens, handbooks on dwarf trees and shrubs.